# Farm Baby Animals
## COLORING BOOK FOR ADULTS
### Vol. 3

Special Art

# The Preview Page:

# THANK YOU SO MUCH FOR PURCHASING THIS BOOK.

Thank you... because **YOU**
give colour and life to our Books...

.. And so we have prepared
**A GIFT** for you!

To get it, use the camera of your phone
to scan the **QR CODE**
on the next page.

We look forward to see you
in our **BIG FAMILY**
of colour lovers.

Good Colouring

*Special Art*

# GET YOUR GIFT!
## OUR 100 BEST COLORING PAGES

Do you have a question or concern? Write to us.
www.specialartbooks.com | support@specialartbooks.com

*Special Art*

# This Book Belongs To:

_____

Choose the colors you love,
Find your favorite drawing
to start with...
And give it life!

# IF YOU LIKED THIS BOOK, HELP US LEAVING A <u>REVIEW</u> ON <u>AMAZON</u> !

*1.* Go to Amazon from your profile and click on "My orders"

*2.* Search this book

*3.* Click on "Write a review for this product"

*4.* Leave us your rating and if you want, add some photos of your fantastic achievements!

## <u>QUICK SOLUTION:</u>
### SCAN YOUR COUNTRY QR CODE BELOW

*SCAN ME*

**UK**  **US**  **CANADA**

THANK YOU VERY MUCH FOR YOUR SUPPORT!

# JOIN OUR FACEBOOK GROUP

✔ Community of Colourists from around the World
✔ Get Free Member-only Content
✔ Share your Artwork
✔ and much more !

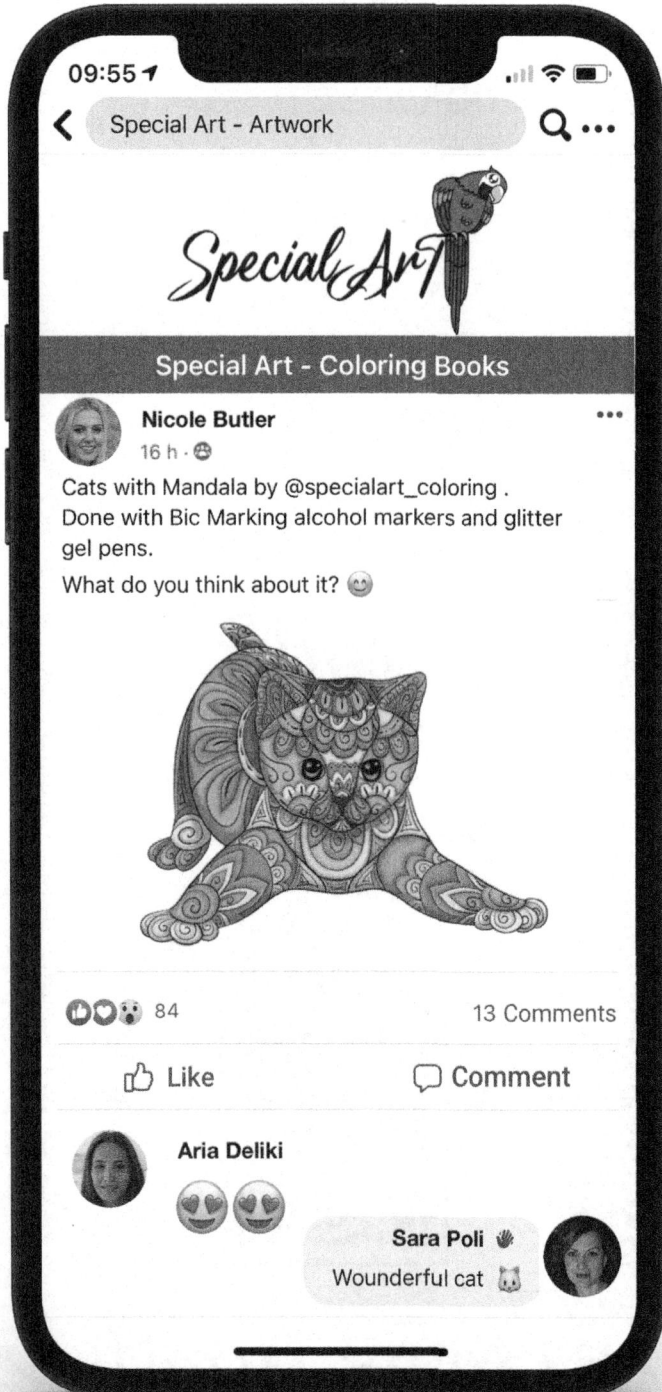

## ENTER NOW

### 1.
Search the group on Facebook:
Special Art – Artwork

### 2.
Join the Group

### 3.
Answer welcome questions

### 4.
You are now part of the community

## OR SCAN WITH YOUR MOBILE PHONE CAMERA
## THE QR CODE BELOW

# FOLLOW US ON INSTAGRAM

✓ To share your artwork with us
✓ See your masterpieces shared on our account
✓ Keep up to date with Contests and News
✓ and much more !

## FOLLOW US NOW

### 1.
Search on Instagram :
@specialart_coloring

### 2.
Follow us

### 3.
Send us a message with photos
of your creations

## TO FIND US IMMEDIATELY SCAN WITH YOUR MOBILE PHONE CAMERA THE QR CODE BELOW

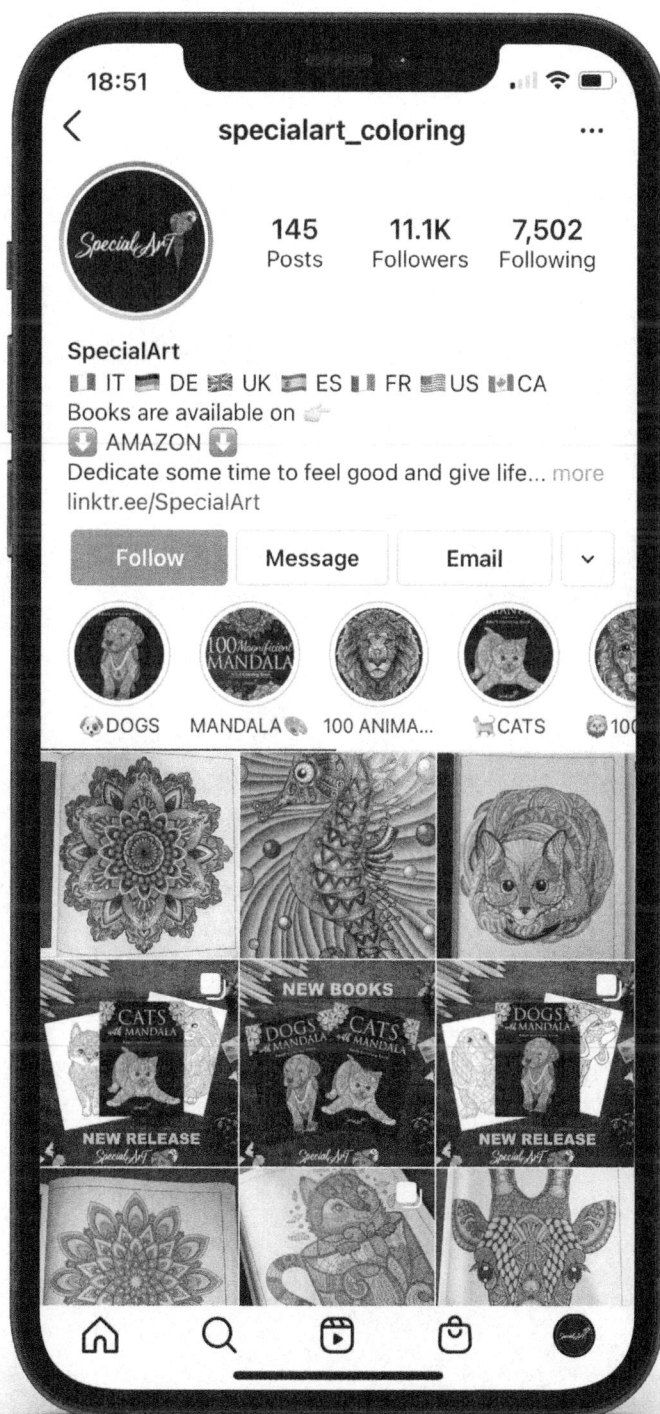

18:51

specialart_coloring

145 Posts  11.1K Followers  7,502 Following

SpecialArt
🇮🇹 IT 🇩🇪 DE 🇬🇧 UK 🇪🇸 ES 🇫🇷 FR 🇺🇸 US 🇨🇦 CA
Books are available on 👉
⬇ AMAZON ⬇
Dedicate some time to feel good and give life... more
linktr.ee/SpecialArt

Follow    Message    Email

DOGS   MANDALA   100 ANIMA...   CATS   100

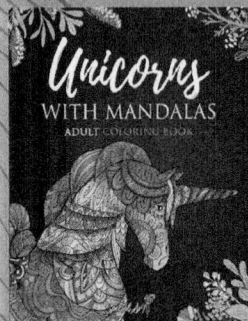

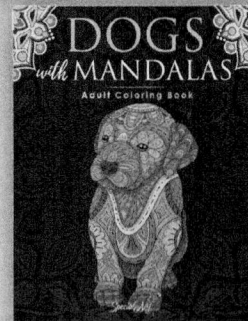

# New Releases

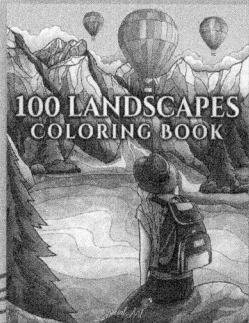

# Tattoos

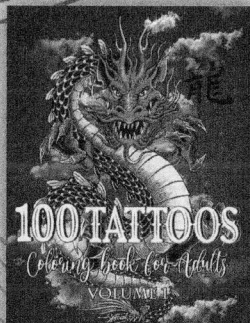

# Beloved

# Enchanted

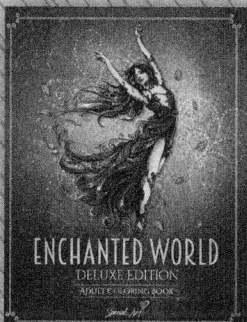
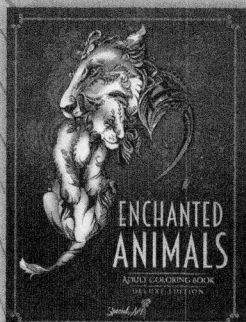

# WE HOPE YOU ENJOYED THIS BOOK!

## Digital Shop
### START YOUR COLORING ADVENTURE

You can find the digital version of this title and many more digital releases on :

# WWW.SPECIALARTBOOKS.COM/SHOP

*SCAN ME*

THANK YOU VERY MUCH FOR CHOOSE ONE OF OUR BOOKS!

Printed in Great Britain
by Amazon

26532990R00037